Theodorus B. Mason

The preservation of life at sea:

A paper read before the American Geographical Society, February 27th,

1879

Theodorus B. Mason

The preservation of life at sea:
A paper read before the American Geographical Society, February 27th, 1879

ISBN/EAN: 9783337716578

Printed in Europe, USA, Canada, Australia, Japan

Cover: Foto ©ninafisch / pixelio.de

More available books at **www.hansebooks.com**

THE

PRESERVATION OF LIFE
AT SEA.

A PAPER READ BEFORE THE

AMERICAN GEOGRAPHICAL SOCIETY,

February 27th, 1879.

BY

THEODORUS B. M. MASON,

LIEUTENANT U. S. NAVY.

FROM THE BULLETIN OF THE SOCIETY.

NEW YORK
1879.

FIRST LINE THROWING EXPERIMENT IN THE UNITED STATES, APRIL, 1849.

THE PRESERVATION OF LIFE AT SEA.

By Lieutenant T. B. M. Mason, United States Navy.

"Measure human sympathy, and you will have taken the dimensions of this subject."*

The subject upon which I have been invited to lecture this evening is one that concerns either directly or indirectly every person in this room. We are all liable at some time to be exposed to the dangers to which I shall refer. My object will be to show you some of the means by which a danger may be met, if by others it has not been prevented. Many of these plans are exceedingly simple, and some of them might be effective if at hand, or in the mind even, in the moment of danger. Few persons are able to invent ideas at that time, but if they have thought over the subject in hours of safety, they may be able not only to save themselves, but all on board.

Perhaps my profession, and the inquiry and correspondence resulting from a paper read by me last year, before the United States Naval Institute, has caused me to overvalue the general interest of the details I have brought together. In enlarging on them before you, I may weary your patience, or in my mode of presenting them I may not do justice to the subject. In asking your indulgence, therefore, I will recall the axiom "Poeta nascitur, orator fit," as specially applicable, in that I have never yet discovered that the role of orator fitted the sailor.

As the description of a number of models and views is necessary

---

*Speech of Hon. Chas. B. Roberts, of Maryland, on the Life-saving Service, House Representatives, June 3d, 1878.

to illustrate the subject, the presentation of which will involve some delay, I trust you will excuse me should I trespass a little beyond the usual time devoted to a paper; and that you will understand that, in presenting or favoring any invention, I shall do so with no personal interest beyond that caused by a conviction that they meet admitted wants, and appear, on examination, to justify the approval they have received from others, either making the life-saving service a specialty, or ordered to test them by constituted authority.

I shall divide my subject under the headings of : personal efforts; aids to personal efforts; aids to combined efforts; preservation of ships; and the life-saving services.

PERSONAL EFFORTS.

The first and most important necessities for preservation, in case of marine accidents, are: *coolness* and a *knowledge of swimming.* Coolness, because it allows you to use your mind, to think what it is best to do; if your mind cannot *tell* you, it will at least *advise* you to keep out of other people's way, and do what others, better informed, may suggest.

Swimming, because it enables you to take care of yourself in the water, and perhaps assist others. It is true that a person who could not walk, could still get about by the aid of crutches, mechanical chairs, and the assistance of others; so a person who cannot swim *may* be saved. There are times, however, when, there being no artificial means at hand, only swimming will save you.

Some here may know the old story of "the philosopher and the boatman," who were crossing a river in a boat. The student had been telling his companion that he had wasted *most* of his life by not knowing how to read and write. Soon after, the boat sinking, the boatman asked if he had learned to swim, and on being informed in the negative, remarked that *he* had wasted the *whole* of his.

Swimming should be learned when young; it is a delightful exercise, affording much amusement, as well as a feeling of security to yourself and to your friends when you are near the water. No young person would consider it a hardship to be taught, but few comparatively now have the opportunity.

Fig. 1. STIFF POSITION, ATTEMPTING TO KEEP HEAD OUT.
Fig. 2. PROPER POSITION FOR SWIMMING.
Fig. 3. FLOATING ON THE BACK.

The great majority of people cannot swim, and, strange as it may seem to you, there are many who follow the sea as a profession who cannot swim a stroke.

There should be swimming tanks attached to all our gymnasiums and schools, where children should be taught to swim as they are now taught, or ought to be taught, calesthenics, dancing and riding.

I have often heard persons say that the best way to teach a child to swim was to pitch it into deep water, and thus force it to look out for itself. This might teach some, but certainly it would be a most risky method, and one not likely to be tried by a parent. One of the first principles in the instruction is not to frighten the pupil. Confidence once destroyed can rarely be replaced.

Some persons teach swimming by supporting the beginner's head. This is a slow and sometimes unsuccessful way, as is that of using life preservers—neither begetting that all-important quality, self-confidence.

At the United States Naval Academy, where all the cadets are taught to swim, the following method is practiced :

When the new cadets enter, each year, they are asked if they can swim; those who say they can are required to demonstrate the fact; if they show proficiency, they are excused from further attendance in this branch, and are allowed to join the older cadets in deep water bathing. The others are excused as they become expert. Those who cannot swim at all, and they form the large majority, are taken in hand by the swimming master.

They are told that the body, being full of air, will float just as an empty bottle does; that the nose is like the spout of the bottle ; it is all that it is necessary to keep out of the water when open; the mouth being kept closed, as is recommended for all other physical exercises. That when they wish to dive, they must cork up the bottle, or rather, hold their breath. That in swimming, the body must be at perfect ease, and they must not attempt to keep more than the nose out of water.

The extra buoyancy of the body depends on the difference between the weight of the water displaced and the body displacing it. Of course any part of the body which is not displacing water has to be carried as dead weight. The extra buoyancy of an ordinary sized man's body is about eleven pounds. The weight of the head is from eight to nine pounds. If they try to push the head up out of water they destroy the easy position of the body, and lose the extra buoyancy. A stout person has greater extra buoyancy than a thin one.

Drowning is caused by allowing the water to replace the air in the body; this causes the body to become heavier than an equal volume of water, and therefore to sink.

The point where a body sinks is generally marked by air bubbles. After sinking the first time, the body sometimes rises to the surface again. This has been known to be repeated even a second time.

Men are drowned by raising their arms above water, the unbuoyed weight of which depresses the head. Other animals have neither notion nor ability to act in a similar manner, and therefore swim naturally. When a man falls into deep water, he will rise to the surface, and will continue there if he does not elevate his hands. If he moves his hands under the water in any way he pleases, his head will rise so high as to allow him free liberty to breathe ; and if he will use his legs as in the act of walking (or rather of walking up-stairs), his shoulders will rise above the water, so that he may use the less exertion with his hands, or apply them to other purposes.

The general principles of swimming having been given, the pupil is placed in a tank, about 70 ft. by 15, shelving from about 1 ft. to 10. In order that the tank may be used in winter, it is furnished with a system of steam pipes for heating the water. The pupil is made to lie out in the shallow water, and shown how to strike out. He is then put into a swimming belt; this is a contrivance consisting of a pole, to the end of which is attached a line; at the end of this line is a belt; this belt passes under each arm and across the chest. The pupil lying in the water is told to strike out. The instructor, supporting him with the pole, walks along at the side of the tank; as soon as he sees that the boy is doing well, he gradually slacks down the pole, which the pupil cannot see, as it is behind him, and cannot feel because he is water-borne. When this point is reached, the instructor informs him that he is swimming. If he gets frightened the instructor supports him again; if not, the ice is broken, and no further trouble is experienced.

Once having learned to swim, learn to float, and also to swim on

5

your back; by this means you can rest yourself, and thus remain in the water a long time. Never remain in from choice, however, after your body begins to feel chilly.

Next learn to swim without using your arms; you have then those members at liberty to assist others.

Never jump in after a person who has fallen into the water unless you are certain that you can be of assistance to him. There are instances of apparently drowning persons rescuing their would-be preservers.

If a person falls overboard and cannot help himself, go to his assistance if you can; if he can help himself, remain where you can assist him out of the water. If you determine to go in, divest yourself of as much of your clothing as possible, especially your shoes. It will be well to mention here that if you are going where you are liable to get into the water, you should have your shoes ready to kick off, or better still, wear low ones.

Having reached the person in danger, if he is not cool and collected, do not approach him so that he can seize you, or he may drag you down with him; either let him exhaust himself, or approach him from the rear, and get him by the hair, or, if he is unprovided with that valuable article, under the chin. Get him on his back, placing yourself in the same position behind him, supporting his head with your hand; strike out for the shore, or wait for other assistance; in this way you can save two or more persons if they are cool subjects. With a very unruly person it is sometimes necessary, for their own good, to use violence; strike them so that they may become insensible. An insensible body, when not filled with water, is very easily handled.

Where a person has gone down, be guided by the bubbles if you cannot see him. Keep your eyes open, and approach him just as directed for surface work.

AIDS TO PERSONAL EFFORTS.

As aids to swimmers, and supports to persons unacquainted with that exercise, thousands of different life-preservers and jackets have been invented.

The best authorities all prefer the cork jacket; rubber and metal are liable to be worn, corroded or punctured, and, therefore, as they are intended to hold air, become useless. Cork is always the same in all climates, and will stand any amount of rough usage. There are many forms of cork jackets or belts, all more or less good.

For a passenger jacket, the requisites are: as much displacement as possible, with a correspondingly small amount of weight. Suppose that a man has an extra buoyancy of ten pounds, and wears a life preserver of a like weight, which only displaces when submerged ten pounds of water, of course he would get no support from it. If, on the contrary, he had one which weighed only one pound, and displaced, when submerged ten pounds, he would have gained nine pounds of extra buoyancy. They should be fitted with a simple system of webbing straps, not leather, and should tie, not buckle. They should be kept, well in view, in places where they can be reached at any time by passengers. In steamers, where passengers sleep, there should always be one jacket near each bunk, besides those on deck. In conspicuous places, near where they are kept, should be printed notices, with drawings, telling and showing how they are to be used, and advising the passenger to examine them closely, and even to put them on, to tie the straps, to fit them, and become thoroughly familiar with them. The straps should always be securely sewed to the jacket,so that they cannot be pulled off or lost. The jacket should be worn just under the arms, these latter thrust through the armholes or suspenders. They should be tied in front of the body; in this position they serve to keep the nose and mouth out of water. Many bodies have been recovered with the preserver about the waist, and, in some cases, about the legs.

Every boat that leaves a ship, or the shore, on service which is not perfectly safe, should have enough life preservers for its crew and passengers. At sea, these should be kept in the boats; these jackets should always be put on. In practice, however, it has generally been found that men pulling take them off, because they interfere with the arm, forcing it to take a position to which they are unaccustomed in rowing; to obviate this I have designed a jacket, which has been made by Mr. W. H. Godfrey, of this city, furnisher to the Navy and Life-saving Service. This gentleman has also kindly lent me the other jackets which I have shown you. A coat life-preserver made of deer's hair has been lent me by Colonel

Fig. 1.

Fig. 2,

Fig. 3,

Fig. 4,

Fig. 1. MAN SWIMMING WITH HAMMOCK.
Fig. 2. CORK LIFE PRESERVER.
Fig. 3. PROPER WAY OF WEARING LIFE PRESERVER.
Fig. 4. MAN SWIMMING WITH LIFE PRESERVER.

Bryson. This coat, which may be worn as an over or watch coat, will support with ease three persons.

Although, on general principles, rubber is not a good material for life saving apparatus ; still the inflatable sleeves and collar of Capt. Ormsbee are so admirably adapted for life saving purposes that I cannot help mentioning them. These would be particularly useful as the private property of travelers, or for use on our beaches in the bathing season.

Merriman's life dress might also be useful if supplied in small numbers, to be worn by seamen in taking a line ashore.

In the Revised Statutes of the United States we find :

"Sec. 4482. Every steam-vessel carrying passengers shall also be provided with a good life-preserver, made of suitable material, for every cabin passenger for which she shall have accommodation, and also a good life-preserver or float for each deck or other class passenger which the inspector's certificate shall allow her to carry, including the officers and crew ; which life-preservers or floats shall be kept in convenient and accessible places on such vessel, in readiness for immediate use in case of accident. "

And again :

"Sec. 4484. Every steamer navigating the ocean, or any lake, bay, or sound of the United States, shall be provided with such numbers of life-preservers as will best secure the safety of all persons on board such vessel in case of disaster."

How these laws are actually carried out, can be seen by any person who travels as far as Brooklyn or Jersey City. The life-preservers are on board, but where are they ? Strapped up under the cabin ceiling, where no one but a giant could possibly reach them, or stuck under the seats, where none but an expert would notice them. In river steamers they are generally stowed in boxes where no one unacquainted with the fact could ever find them. In ocean steamers they are often kept in some out-of-the-way locker. In men-of-war the small number allowed can usually be found in the furthest corner of the yeoman's store-room.

Another, and most effective means of supporting the body in the water, is the adaptation of the bed and other cushions for use as life-preservers. This idea would furnish economical owners with life-preservers, where they had such contrivances, without additional expense. It would economize space, always a coveted article aboard ship. By their superior size and greater buoyancy, they would support a person in the water better than a jacket.

Every person on board must be provided with a bed of some kind, whether it be the hammock of the sailor or the bunk of the passenger and officer.

For years officers in our own and the English service have been agitating this subject. The great difficulty which all workers in this as well as in all other life-preserving projects have had to encounter, is the unwillingness of those who are in safety on shore to provide for the dangers to which they themselves or others may be exposed at sea. The originator of the idea was probably Rear Admiral Ryder, R. N. In our country, Mr. R. B. Forbes has been indefatigable in urging its adoption, and I would state that Mr. Forbes is and has been one of our most zealous workers. To his energy and perseverance many persons owe their lives to-day. Commander Cyprian Bridge, R. N., found by experiment that the sailors' hammock, carefully lashed, supported seven men in the water for several minutes—four men for almost an hour. Captain Arthur Wilnshurst, R. N., found that a hammock with a six-pound shot suspended from one end—a most trying test—floated for five minutes. The buoyancy of the hammocks was found to be at first 114 lbs. The same shot suspended from the centre was supported nine minutes. The ticking was then oiled, and the hammock supported the weight two and a half hours.

It can readily be imagined that a hammock capable of thus supporting a dead weight would be of great assistance to a man. Had this fact been known to the officers of many of the men-of-war which have sunk suddenly, the loss of life would have been much smaller.

By filling the mattress with cork shavings, which are very cheap, generally being thrown away, additional buoyancy may be obtained. A mattress six feet by four, stuffed with this material, weighed 20 lbs.; its buoyancy was sufficient to support eighty pounds, dead weight, indefinitely. The cost was one-half that of a hair one. A mattress stuffed with granulated cork, 5 ft. 6 in. by 1 ft. 10 in., and 3 in. deep (hammock size), weighing thirteen pounds and having a buoyancy of sixty pounds, is now issued to the men of the Royal Navy.

Mr. Forbes writes that a cotton canvas hammock, containing a mattress stuffed with cork shavings, tested by Lieut.-Cmdr. O'Neil, U. S. N., sustained sixty-two pounds one hour and five minutes, and thirty-two pounds indefinitely. The same hammock, placed in a closely woven water-proofed cotton canvas bag, had its buoyancy increased about four times. Twenty hammocks thus provided, lashed together with a frame-work of spars, would support a 2,000 pound anchor, and one hundred would carry the heaviest anchor used in the navy.

Cocoa fibre has been used as a filling, but I have been unable to obtain any reliable information in regard to it.

Deer's hair, on account of its extreme lightness and great displacement, is also used.

The samples which I have are furnished by Col. Bryson, of the Deer Hair Manufacturing Company. The mattress, which weighs only 5 lbs., is very buoyant. This style of mattress has been used in the Government and Merchant services for several years with excellent results.

A mattress stuffed with felt has just been adopted by the Navy Department and issued for trial. It has also been approved and recommended by a board ordered by the Chief of the Steamboat Inspection Service. This is a step in the right direction, and could steamship companies be made to see that their own interests would be advanced by providing such means, and advertising it, just as hotels have provided fire-escapes and apparatus, a great stride would have been taken.

This mattress is invented and made by Mr. II. D. Ostermoor, of this city. The board of naval officers who tested it at Washington report that "The mattress consists of several sheets or thicknesses of raw cotton, which had been subjected to a great heat, to remove all possible trace of vegetable oils, and then while under pressure to a process which renders the fibres impervious to water or dampness."

A bunk mattress of this kind supported one man weighing 150 pounds, who stood upon it, and a dead weight of fifty pounds of iron, without sinking enough to wet its upper side. It supported two such men, only wetting the soles of their shoes. After twenty-four hours' floating, the ticking having become saturated, the inside was examined and found to be totally untouched by moisture—the extreme outer fibres of the outer sheets being barely touched by the dampness. Heavy weights were then used to sink it, and it remained under water forty-eight hours ; upon being examined at the end of this time it was found that the moisture had penetrated between the sheets, the interior of the sheets themselves being entirely free from dampness. The mattress was then dried, when the usual softness and springiness was observed to return to the material. So well pleased were the board with the comfort and cheapness of the mattress, that they recommended it even for shore use. They have, however, already been used for a long time on shore, and even afloat. Alexandre's New York, Havana and Mexican Mail Steamship Line has used them for two years. Pullman uses them in his sleeping-cars, and uses the material for stuffing the cushions of his palace cars, and for the cars of the Metropolitan Elevated Railroad. They are used in many of the Hospitals and Public Institutions. All who have used them testify in highest terms as to their softness, their not lumping, and their cleanliness—there being no animal oil or fat in them.

The objection to mattresses stuffed with cork is their hardness, and sogginess after being in the water for some time. To those with waterproof covers, their smell.

A felt-stuffed pillow weighing three and a half pounds, on which was placed thirty pounds of iron, is reported by the steamboat inspectors to have floated eight days.

A chair cushion would therefore support a man in the water with the greatest ease.

A mattress such as is used in the bunks of vessels fitted, at my proposition, with handles or beckets round the sides, would support several persons in the water. One person may lie on the mattress; the straps being secured over the body prevent a possibility of rolling off. This would be most valuable for children, women, and persons injured during the accident. The handles of one side and one end are provided with snap hooks, so that a number of mattresses may be secured together, to form a raft, which could be improved by the addition of spars and a lashing. The cushions are also to be fitted with handles, the smaller ones being fitted with straps, so that they may be converted into life-jackets. The mattresses intended for

Fig. 1.

Fig. 2.

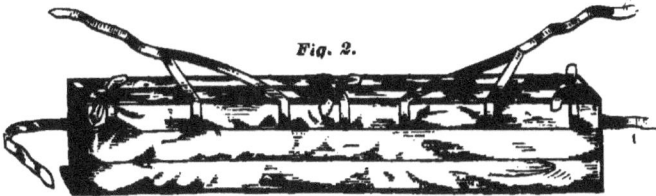

Fig. 3.

Fig. 1. FELT BUNK MATTRESS FITTED WITH HANDLES AND HOOKS.

Fig. 2. FELT HAMMOCK MATTRESS FITTED WITH STRAPS AS LIFE PRESERVERS

Fig 3 DEER HAIR MATTRESS, WITH END FITTED AS A LIFE PRESERVER.

hammocks, or as second mattresses in bunks, are fitted with straps and loops, so that they may be doubled over and form life-jackets. When a lashed hammock is to be used as a life preserver, which would occur when a man-of-war was sinking in the day-time, the clews are to be brought together and secured. This forms a ring-buoy, which is placed around the body, under the arms.

In order that life-saving appliances may be useful in sudden emergencies, they should be numerous, so that in some form they may be at hand in every part of the vessel likely to be inhabited by the crew and passengers. Notices should be posted, telling what may be used; it is not only necessary to have them about, but attention must be called to them. In speaking of this with a steamship man, he objected, on the ground that if too many precautions were taken, and too much publicity given to such things, they would frighten away travelers. Does the knowledge that one is provided with a good fire-escape, to get out of a house in case of fire, prevent one from going there to live ? I think, on the contrary, that wise travelers would be attracted by such precautions. The first duty of a traveler embarking, if only to cross the river, should be to look about for them ; if he does not see them he should insist upon the employees showing them to him ; if he does not succeed he had better go ashore and patronize some other line.

If people would only be as anxious and pertinacious about their safety as they are about their comfort, there would be no need of laws enforcing the carrying of life appliances; companies and owners, in order to secure crews and passengers, would be forced in competition to adopt them.

A person who is going to travel sometimes goes months before-hand to engage a good state-room, and then pays the steward a large fee for a good seat at the table. What does he do towards his preservation ? Does he insist upon being shown a certified plan of the vessel, displaying her collision bulkheads, and a list of her fire and life-saving appliances ?

Does he insist upon the agent's marking on his ticket what boat he is to go in, or what raft he is to look to for safety, taking care to find out how many others are detailed for the same conveyance, and what its capacity really is ?

Does he ask whether the mattresses are buoyant, and whether life preservers are provided at hand, and not stowed away below?

Does he, when he goes aboard, go on deck and find out where the boat or raft is, and how he is to get to it day or night; how he can assist in getting it out, or lowering it; whether it contains oars, life belts, provisions, and water; if not, where they are kept; whether an officer and crew are detailed for it?

Does he go down to his room, examine his mattress, and find out how it works; take down his life-preserver; read the instructions; put it on, and fit the straps to suit his size, making himself familiar with it, so that he can put it on in the dark?

Not a bit of it; 999 look out for their seats at table, see what flowers or delicacies their friends have sent, get their chairs all right, and then lounge about until, mayhap, father Neptune causes them to bow to him. When the hour of danger comes, it is too late to do what might have made them then cool, self-possessed, and self-reliant.

If men would not ship in vessels where they are not provided with proper appliances, owners would be forced to spend a few hundred dollars, and provide them.

If it is impossible to provide these facilities without augmenting the receipts, no sensible traveler, however, would growl at paying a dollar or two more to insure his life.

There are many lines of steamers running between this port and Europe, all more or less poorly provided. Public opinion should force them to do better. There is one line which unites us to a great sister Republic which has been unfortunate, and which, having profited by its experience, is probably the best provided to-day. There is another line which, for a long series of years, by good seamanship and good luck, has never had an accident. Are they as well provided? Many of you, who have traveled intelligently, can probably answer this question.

Another life-saving contrivance is what is called the life buoy, intended to be dropped or thrown to a person in the water by those on board. The larger forms are carried over the stern. They are dropped by some mechanical contrivance. For day work they are sometimes provided with little red flags, so that they may be the more readily seen. At night they are distinguished by a light of some kind. In our service we use portfire for this light ; this has to be lit by a percussion lock and cap, which is fired as the buoy is ˙dropped ; this sometimes misses, and the water sometimes extinguishes the light. The French Government has adopted the Silas apparatus. The light in this is caused by the ignition of the gas of phosphurated calcium. Phosphurated calcium, which is common chalk, acted upon when at great heat by the fumes of heated phosphorus. The product, which is brown in color, and in lumps of the shape into which the chalk was broken, when thrown into water, or acted upon by great dampness, gives off a gas which ignites with a brilliant flame on combining with the air. On account of this peculiar quality, it must be kept in an air-tight case, which has been previously thoroughly dried ; in this state it is harmless. For use, the receiver, which is of glass generally, is placed in a tube placed vertically through the centre of the float; this tube is open at either end. As the buoy drops a plunger is released, which opens the receiver ; the water, coming up through one end of the tube, acts upon the calcium, liberating the gas, which, passing up through the tube, and escaping through the upper ends, unites with the air and becomes inflamed. Of course, water will not extinguish this light. A person dropping a buoy to one who has fallen overboard from forward, should wait until he is as near to him as possible. When the person is already astern, let the buoy go as quickly as possible. If the buoy is too far from the person, it may never be reached by him. The wind or current also act sometimes to carry it away from him. Mr. Forbes reports very excellent results in preventing this by attaching to each buoy a little canvas cone, which acts as a drag or sea anchor. About the decks there should be a number of ring buoys, which a cool person may pitch almost into the hands of a person overboard. When these are not at hand, gratings, chairs, or any floatable object should be used.

The ring buoy is another form, and should always be carried in considerable numbers about the decks. The two which I have here this evening are rather large ones. One is of granulated cork, very heavy, and liable to become water-soaked ; the other of deer's hair, very light and buoyant.

Few small ·life-saving contrivances are intended to support the whole dead weight of the body; they are intended to be held on to. Never attempt to climb on top of a life-buoy, for instance ; it will support you as long as you keep your body submerged.

The following directions for restoring the apparently drowned are from the latest instructions issued by our Life Saving Service; they are those of Dr. Howard.

Where you can do so, send immediately for a regular medical practitioner.

RULE I.—*Arouse the Patient.*—Unless in danger of freezing, do not move the patient, but instantly expose the face to a current of fresh air, wipe dry the mouth and nostrils, rip the clothing, so as to expose the chest and waist, and give two or three quick smarting slaps on the stomach and chest with the open hand. If the patient does not revive, proceed thus :

RULE II.—*To Draw off Water, &c., from the Stomach and Chest.*—If the jaws are clenched, separate them, and keep the mouth open by placing between the teeth a cork, or small bit of wood ; turn the patient on the face, a large bundle of tightly rolled clothing being placed beneath the stomach, and press heavily over it for half a minute, or so long as fluids flow freely from the mouth.

RULE III.—*To Produce Breathing.*—Clear the mouth and throat of mucus by introducing into the throat the corner of a handkerchief wrapped closely around the forefinger ; turn the patient on the back, the roll of clothing being so placed as to raise the pit of the stomach above the level of any other portion of the body. If there be another person present, let him, with a piece of dry cloth, hold the tip of the tongue out of one corner of the mouth (this prevents the tongue from pulling back and obstructing the windpipe), and with the other hand grasp both wrists, and keep the arms forcibly stretched back above the head, thereby increasing the prominence of the ribs, which tends to enlarge the chest. The two last-named positions are not, however, essential to success. Kneel beside or astride the patient's hips, and with the balls of the thumbs resting on either side of the pit of the stomach, let the fingers fall into the grooves between the short ribs, so as to afford the best grasp of the waist. Now, using your knees as a pivot, throw all your weight forward on your hands, and at the same time squeeze the waist between them, as if you wished to force everything in the chest

Fig. 1.

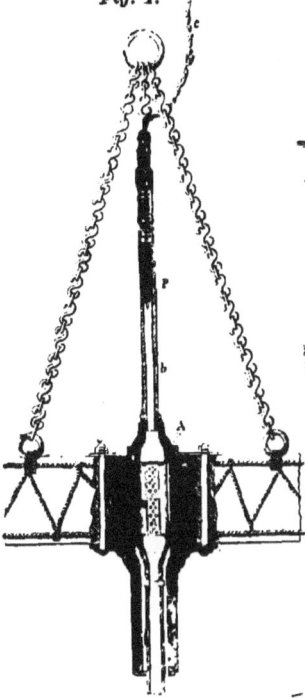

Fig. 3.

Fig. 4.

Fig. 2.

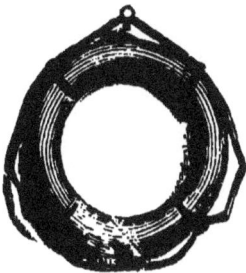

Fig. 1. SILAS LIFE BUOY.

Fig 2 RING BUOY.

Fig. 3. SHOWING EJECTION OF WATER FROM BODY.

Fig 4. SHOWING METHOD OF RESTORING RESPIRATION.

upward out of the mouth; deepen the pressure while you can count
slowly one, two, three; then suddenly let go with a final push,
which springs you back on your first kneeling position. Remain
erect on your knees while you can count one, two, three; then
repeat the same motions as before, at a rate gradually increased
from four or five to fifteen times in a minute, and continue thus this
bellows movement, with the same regularity that is observable in
the natural motions of breathing which you are imitating. If natural breathing be not restored after a trial of the bellows movement
for three or four minutes, then, without interrupting the artificial
respiration, turn the patient a second time on the stomach, as
directed in Rule II, rolling the body in the opposite direction from
that in which it was first turned, for the purpose of freeing the air
passages from any remaining water. Continue the artificial respiration from one to four hours, or until the patient breathes; and for a
while after the appearance of returning life, carefully aid the first
short gasps until deepened into full breaths. Continue the drying
and rubbing, which should have been unceasingly practised from
the beginning, taking care not to interfere with the means employed
to produce breathing. Thus, the limbs of the patient should be .
rubbed, always in an upward direction towards the body, with firm
grasping pressure and energy, using the bare hands, dry flannels or
handkerchiefs, and continuing the friction under the blankets, or
over the dry clothing. The warmth of the body can also be pro-
moted by the application of hot flannels to the stomach and arm-
pits, bottles or bladders of hot water, heated bricks, stones, &c., to
the limbs and soles of the feet.

RULE IV.—*After-Treatment.*—*Externally:* As soon as breathing
is established, let the patient be stripped of all wet clothing,
wrapped in blankets only, put to bed comfortably warm, but with
a free circulation of fresh air, and left to perfect rest. *Internally:*
Give a little brandy and hot water, or other stimulant at hand,
every ten or fifteen minutes during the first hour, and as often
thereafter as may seem expedient. *Later manifestations:* After
reaction is fully established there is great danger of congestion of
the lungs, and if perfect rest is not maintained for at least forty-
eight hours, it sometimes occurs that the patient is seized with great
difficulty of breathing, and death is liable to follow unless imme-

diate relief is afforded. In such cases apply a large mustard plaster over the breast. If the patient gasps for breath before the mustard takes effect, assist the breathing by carefully repeating the artificial respiration.

An eminent authority, Dr. Labordette, the Supervising Surgeon of the Hospital of Lisieux, in France, appears to have established the fact that the clenching of the jaws and semi-contraction of the fingers, which have hitherto been considered signs of death, are, in fact, evidences of remaining vitality. After numerous experiments with apparently drowned persons, and also with animals, he concludes that these are only signs accompanying the first stage of suffocation by drowning, the jaws and hands becoming relaxed when death ensues (the "rigor mortis" occurs later after the temporary relaxation here referred to). This being so, the mere clenching of the jaws and semi-contraction of the hands must not be considered as reasons for the discontinuance of efforts to save life, but should serve as a stimulant to vigorous and prolonged efforts to quicken vitality. Persons engaged in the task of resuscitation are, therefore, earnestly desired to take hope and encouragement for the life of the sufferer from the signs above referred to, and to continue their endeavors accordingly. In a number of cases Dr. Labordette restored to life persons whose jaws were so firmly clenched that, to aid respiration, their teeth had to be forced apart with iron instruments.

Directions for restoring the apparently drowned should be legibly printed, with accompanying plates, and posted in every steamer, ferry-house, and public building near the water, on wharves and bridges—in fact, everywhere—that they might be made useful either to the idler, or the person desiring to refer to them. In England the Royal Humane Society has adopted this device; why cannot our own Life Saving Benevolent Society do the same?

AIDS TO COMBINED EFFORTS.

Under this head we will class all the life-preservers coming between the personal float and the ship, whether used from the shore or from vessels. Ordinary pulling boats are generally, except in fine weather, of little use in saving life. They are too often, especially in the navy, built for speed instead of safety. A boat, to be of use in bad weather, or in approaching a rock, or surf bound shore, should be fitted so as to be easily gotten out, or lowered, very buoyant, unupsetable, unsinkable, and easy to be handled and beached.

For ordinary boats, of which by-the-bye it would be almost impossible to carry enough to safely transport all the passengers and crew of large vessels, in selecting a lowering apparatus, we have to be governed to a certain extent by other necessary qualities. A sea-going vessel cannot carry her boats rigged out, as they would certainly be carried away in anything like a bad sea. In a vessel rolling very badly, if they were not carried away, by filling with water they might prevent the vessel from righting. Some ships cannot even carry their boats on the rail, but have to take them inboard. In coming alongside of other vessels, or docks, it is necessary that the boats should be rigged in. In most vessels this is done by first hoisting the boat by means of davits, or derricks. If the boat is to come inboard, or on the rail, these are turned, and the boat lowered into chocks, or into a cradle. So far the operation is of no importance, as there is no hurry, and plenty of men and mechanical contrivances are at hand. When, however, the boat has to be gotten out, its whole weight has generally to be raised out of the chocks, or cradle, under the most disadvantageous circumstances. It has then to be turned outboard, quite a complicated manœuvre, and lowered with great care and at great risk of being dashed to pieces against the side, or capsized before the tackles are unhooked. In order to obviate all these difficulties, it is necessary to have a boat lowering apparatus, and then a boat detaching one.

There are many different forms of both of these, but I am sorry to say that even the best are more often found in books and models than in actual practice. They are expensive, or at least more so than nothing—this is enough to condemn them.

Mr. Forbes has sent me a contrivance which he recommends most highly, and which, I should judge, must be very excellent, and as cheap as an ordinary davit. There are two upright stanchions built into the rail; hinged to these, at the height of the deck, are two pieces which act as the arms of derricks. The upper ends are connected by a fore and aft piece; on this fore and aft piece, which also acts as a strong back for the boat, are the tackles. To prevent this arm from going out too far when out, or coming in too far when in, there is a length of chain permanently attached to the head of the stanchion. To prevent the arm from coming in when out, and going out when in, there is a rigid hook bar. A chain pennant, to the end of which a tackle is fitted, is used to bring the arm to a vertical position, and lower it either in or out. The important feature is, that when in the boat can be rigged out by being pushed upon, no raising being necessary. The tackles, when the boat is hoisted, are replaced by single ropes, so that the boat can be easily lowered. The boat-detaching apparatus of Ensign Bradley A. Fiske, U. S. N., adopted for use in the navy, works very well. The object of a detacher is, to let go both ends of the boat at once as she approaches the water; this must be done by one person, placed at some central point. It may even be necessary, when the ship is rolling heavily, to let go half way down, to prevent being smashed against the side. A ship's boats should be, if possible, of the life-boat type ; if they are not, they should at least be fitted with air tanks under the thwarts, or cork paddings round the rail outside. The rudders should always be kept shipped. An oar is preferable to a rudder, if properly shipped, when quick work is to be done. There are many different types of life-boat, from the large steam ones used by the English and French to the small, very small, zinc ones used aboard our river craft. All are more or less good. They are made as light as possible, are given great displacement, and consequently buoyancy. They are made self-bailing, by being provided with valves in their bottoms, or even by having the bottoms almost entirely open to the sea. Boats for pulling, quick handling, and beaching, should be fitted with centre-boards, and without keels.

As we have stated, it is almost impossible for a large vessel to carry enough boats for all the people she may have on board. Other contrivances must be at hand in the way of rafts. The Rider life raft is the one which seems best to meet the requirements of the case. These have been adopted in our service. The model is furnished by the present makers to the navy, the " Gondola Life-boat and Raft Company." The advantage of this contrivance is, that it affords a very large amount of buoyancy when submerged. It is very light, and when not inflated takes up but little room, a coveted

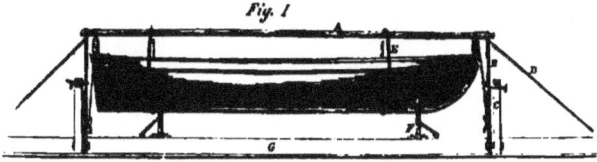

Fig. 1

Fig. 2

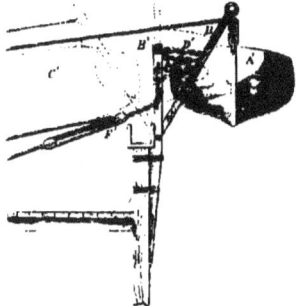

Apparatus for Lowering, dropping, hoisting in
and hoisting Boats in a Seaway.

Fig. 3.

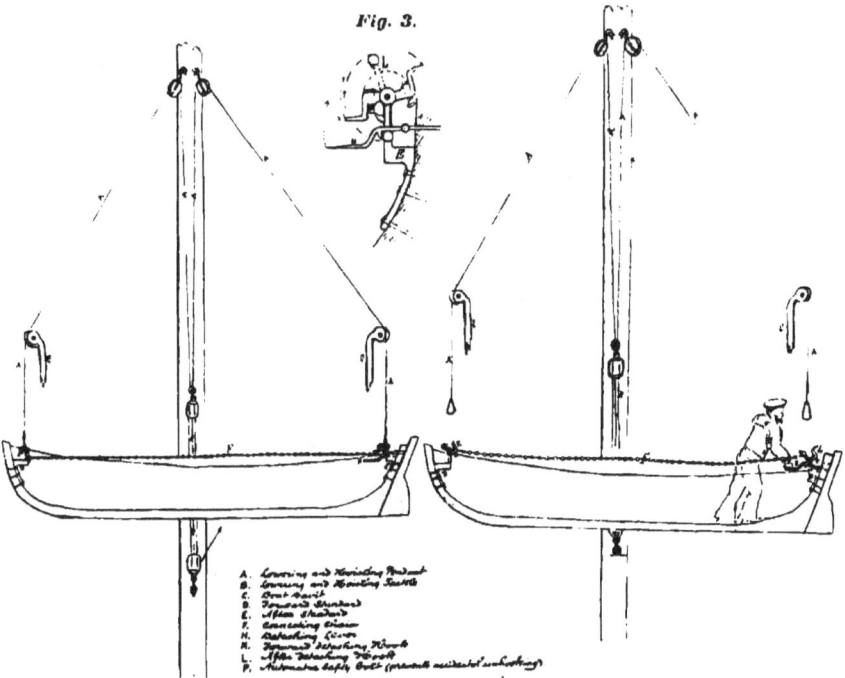

A. Lowering and hoisting Pendant
B. Lowering and hoisting Tackle
C. Boat Davit
D. Forward Standard
E. After Standard
F. Connecting Chain
H. Detaching Cover
M. Forward Detaching Hook
L. After Detaching Hook
P. Automatic safety Bolt (prevents accidental unhooking)

Fig. 1. SIDE VIEW OF FORBES' DAVITS.
Fig. 2. END VIEW OF FORBES' DAVITS.
Fig. 3. FISKE'S DETACHING APPARATUS.

article aboard ship. Many of these can be carried in the space required for one boat. They can be put on top of deck-houses, lashed under forecastles and bridges. They are quickly fitted for use, and can be launched from the deck without difficulty, on account of their lightness. Afloat, they carry a large number of people, are easily handled, and can be taken through a surf with all the safety of a life-boat.

Admiral Ammen, who recently addressed this society on the subject of the Isthmus Surveys, is the inventor of a bolsa very similar in form to the rubber one, but with the floats made up of staves, like a barrel. In the water it is excellent, but it does not stow as well aboard ship.

In making rafts, hammocks or mattresses, if made available by some of the methods already suggested, would be of the greatest utility.

It would also be important to have all the doors and other movable woodwork given extra buoyancy by having air boxes fitted in the panels.

It has been suggested that the decks of houses and bridges should be fitted with air boxes between the beams, and attached to the vessel by heavy keys, which could be knocked away in an emergency with mauls, which should be kept at hand. Such an arrangement, if it did not interfere with the solidity of the ship itself, might save many valuable lives.

The collapsible boats of the Rev. E. L. Berthon, an English clergyman, have been adopted by the British Government. They are of canvas fitted over a frame, which opens or shuts something like an umbrella, thus allowing a large number to be carried without occupying much space.

On most of our coasts the life-saving crews prefer to use boats built like the fishing boats which they are accustomed to, and as actual experiments have proved that they are best, owing to the peculiar shallowness of water, the long distances to be traveled before reaching the scene of action, and the necessity of taking on nearly raw crews every winter, this form has been adopted.

The crew of a vessel stranded should only leave her in their own boats as a last resort. They should establish the line communication, to be referred to hereafter, or wait for the boat from the shore.

Few sailors are good surfmen ; in fact, it is a profession by itself. Not being surfmen, they cannot prevent their boats being upset or pitch-poled (thrown end over end) when they get in the surf. If they do have to use their boats, they must anchor outside of the surf and get up a line communication from there. If it is absolutely necessary to go through the surf, a flexible raft made of hammocks or mattresses, which will bend to the action of the wave and not pitch-pole or capsize, will be found much safer than a boat. We will not attempt here to give the proper method of handling a boat in the surf.

SHIPS.

The dangers to which ships are usually subjected are : burning colliding, upsetting and stranding. Much can be done to protect the ship against all of these dangers, and it should be the traveler's duty to assure himself, before engaging passage, that all these precautions have been taken. This could easily be shown by a sworn statement and plans, with a heavy penalty attached to deception. At present the competition is so great between companies that they have to do everything as cheaply as possible. There is not to-day one single vessel sailing or steaming from this port or any other which is properly provided. If a law were passed, either by constituted authority or the good sense of the traveling public, they would all start fair in the race for safety. We see references made to water-tight compartments and collision bulkheads. They do not exist, in practice, any more than we can call the walls of this room water-tight. Some of the vessels are provided with partitions, which might be made water-tight, but not at the moment when they are needed. To be of use, they must be so beforehand. There must not be a single opening in them below the water-line, and even for some distance above it, as the line of floatation would be raised, by the filling of one of the compartments, to a considerable extent. A very small hole, such as a sluice-valve, takes from a partition any claim to be called water-tight. Any one who has studied hydrostatics knows what a quantity of water can pass through a small orifice in a short space of time. Compartments must be absolutely water-tight. They must be several stories high,

Fig. 1.

Fig. 2.

Fig. 3.

Fig. 4.

Fig. 1. THE LATEST ARRANGEMENT OF WATER TIGHT BULK HEADS.

Fig. 2. EFFECT OF BULK HEADS NOT BEING HIGH ENOUGH, WHEN WATER LINE IS RAISED BY A COMPARTMENT FILLING.

Fig. 3. NECESSITY OF SMALL COMPARTMENTS AT EXTREMITIES.

Fig. 4. BENEFIT OF HORIZONTAL PARTITIONS.

and the decks or floors of these stories must be absolutely water and air-tight. The bottoms must be double. The whole under water, and up to at least six feet above the water, part of a ship, must be like a honeycomb. The bulkheads must run fore and aft as well as athwart ship. The engine and boiler-rooms must be in compartments as well as the rest of the ship. This can easily be done if it must be done. The shafts can be made to work through watertight bearings through the partitions, just as they do in the stern-post. The very part of the ship occupied now by an immense open space, is the one which we should most subdivide. The forward compartments should be very small, so as not to lift the screw and rudder out of the water when they filled. The coal should be stowed well up on both sides of the engines and boilers to protect them, and also to be at hand, so that no excuse could be made of difficulty of getting at it on account of the bulkheads. Each compartment 'should have a separate pump, and each of these pumps should be fitted to work for water or air. None of the engines for working these pumps should be placed down in the engine-room where a fire might cut them off. Each compartment should be fitted with an electric fire alarm, and if possible with an automatic extinguisher. Cargo should all be packed in waterproof cases, or, better still, in barrels. The compartments being full of such packages would admit but little water. What did come in could be forced out by turning on the air-pump. The steering gear of all ships should be worked by steam and hand, and the helmsman placed forward close to the officer of the deck, who should be there also. A second apparatus should be placed aft in case of accident. The officer of the watch should be able to stop the engines himself without leaving the bridge. This can be done by electricity, and has been worked successfully aboard a French man-of-war. There should be an ample supply of fire extinguishers, buckets and axes always at hand. There should be permanent steam or water pipes such as are fitted in hotels and large buildings, by which steam or water could be sent to every part of the ship by syphon or other pumps. Each apartment should be provided with a tap to this pipe, and a piece of hose long enough to reach any part of it.

In case of meeting a vessel at sea, in the daytime, there is generally but little danger of collision, but collisions have occurred ;

therefore we must guard against them. The great cause of collision is a want of knowledge of what the other ship is doing or going to do. In other words, how she has her helm. This could easily be remedied by having a semaphore at the mainmast head, similar to those used on railroads; this to be connected automatically with the steering wheel. As port is always designated by red (let us suppose because port wine is of a reddish color) and starboard by green, when the helm was put to port, the red arm would rise in proportion to the angle of the rudder; when the helm was amidships neither arm would be up; when the helm was put to starboard the green arm would rise. In this way, on any side, the position of the helm could be seen.

At night lights might be attached to these arms, or the officer of the watch might carry in his starboard and port pockets a green and a red signal, which he could burn in the same way. It was ordered at one time by the English Board of Trade that this light system should be adopted in the following manner : That a light of the color of the side to which the helm was put should be shown on deck on approaching, or a little ways up the rigging of a vessel. A vessel always carries, or should always carry, at night (some owners and captains are so mean that they attempt even to evade this law, by not carrying their lights when they are clear of the harbor authorities—men-of-war should be empowered to capture every vessel found without lights), on the starboard side, well forward, a green light, so protected that it cannot be seen abaft the beam ; on the port side, a red light. A steamer carries at her foremast head a white light. In practice, when the helm signal was exhibited, confusion arose, because all the colored lights were so nearly on a line. This caused the order to be rescinded. I propose that the lights carried by the officer of the watch shall be of the system which is now coming into operation for general signals—that is, that the light shall be projected into the air by being fired out of a pistol or case. This would prevent all confusion, and it could then be seen on all sides. The signal lights which I have here are made by Mr. Edward S. Linton, and would be just the things to carry out the idea. They are cylinders stopped at one end, and containing any number of stars that may be desired. These stars are projected one after the other, at equal intervals, to a great height in the air, where

Plate 7.

E.P.Linton's Signal proposed for use with this system.

M = Powder.
MM = Time Fuse.
MMM = Star Composition.
7 = Quick Match.

Signal Rocket with Friction Primer.

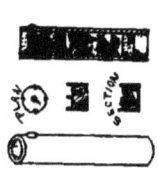

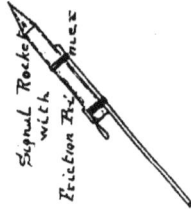

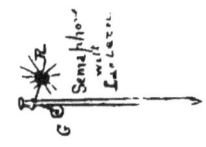

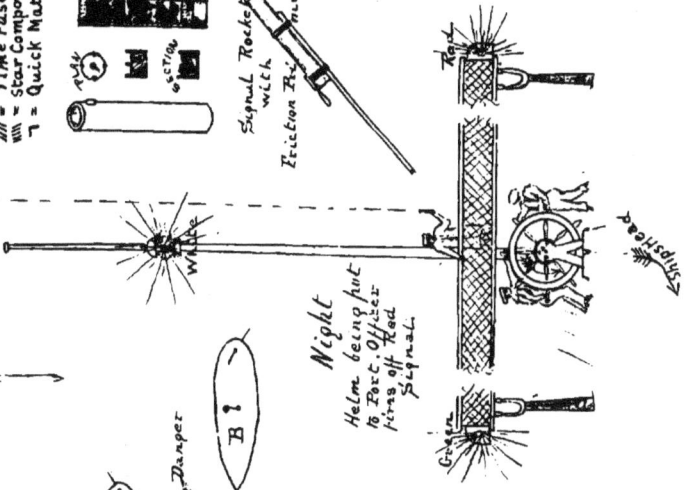

Night
Helm being put to Port Officer fires off Red Signal.

Shiphead.

Proposed method to lessen the liabilities of collision

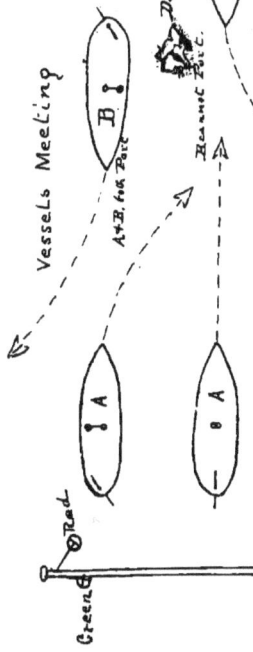

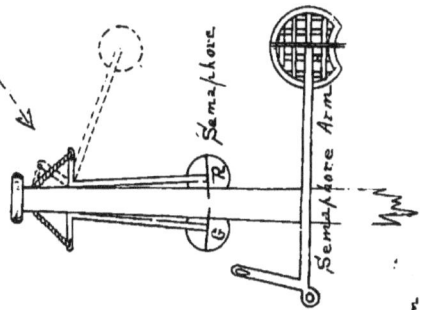

Vessels Meeting

Danger

A & B, his Port

Recent Port.

Day

Semaphore

Semaphore Arm

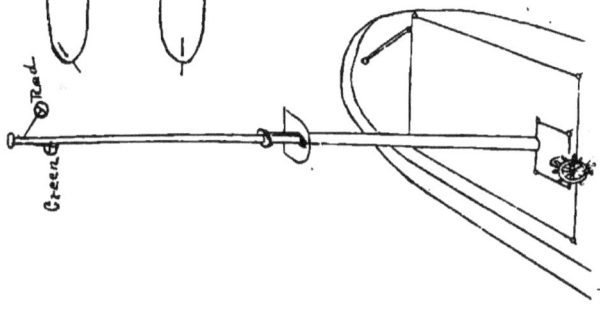

Shows how Signal Semaphore works automatically with the helm.

they burn. The machine is put in operation by striking the cap against a hard substance, such as the bridge, rail, or deck. By carrying these in the two side pockets, or in pouches on a belt, they come naturally to the hand, which is instinctively put in motion on giving the order to the helmsman. They are drawn out and fired instantaneously by the person giving the order, so that the factor of error liable to occur by having another person bungle, and perhaps break a lantern, is also eliminated. The rocket which I have here, made for me by the same gentleman, is fitted so as to be fired by merely pulling the primer tape, and thus doing away with the necessity of looking for a light and perhaps having it blown or washed out.

An electric light at the masthead would do much to prevent collisions and stranding, by lighting up a vessel and its surroundings. Such a light could be supplied with electricity by the engines, and put in operation or extinguished by the officer of the deck himself. It will probably seem that I am multiplying too much the duties of the officer of the deck ; but I think that any one who has ever occupied that by no means enviable position in time of danger, will agree that, being placed in a central position with a good all-round view, the more all different operations can be brought under your own personal control the better. It is getting more difficult every year to get intelligent assistants.

Having enumerated some of the general precautions that might be taken, let us see how they would apply to our cited dangers.

Fire, by localizing it by bulkheads ; by giving the alarm by automatic means ; by subduing the fire by extinguishers, automatic or portable, or with steam water and compressed air.

Collisions, by preventing them by the precautions proposed ; if not prevented, localizing the damage by bulkheads and compartments. The vessel would also be strengthened to resist the shock by the network of partitions. The pump and air pumps would free the compartments, the waterproof cases prevent the goods being saturated. All persons likely to hold positions on board a vessel where they will be required to look out for lights, should be thoroughly examined in regard to Daltonism or color blindness. Recent researches in the German and French navies prove that many persons are thus affected. Upsetting must be prevented, in the first place, by the naval architect when he plans his vessel; by the stevedore when he loads her, and by the seaman when he handles her. Although within the province of this paper, our limited time and your already overtaxed patience will not permit me to go more fully into this subject than to call your attention, if you are professional men, to the excellent new method of Mr. Forbes for reducing top hamper, and to the fact that when the rolling period of the ship and the period of the sea approach very closely, it is better to heave to or change your course.

Stranding must be prevented by navigation, by continual sounding and reference to the chart when approaching the shore. As under the previous head, I must omit the interesting technical facts connected with improved compasses and sounding apparatus, especially those Captain Belknap and Lieut.-Commanders Sigsbee and Jewell. Improved methods of approaching dangerous places, such as the method proposed by Lieutenant Truedell, of the French Navy, now employed as a captain in the service of the Transatlantic Company, for entering the harbor of New York in foul weather. There is one point, however, referring to this head and that of collision, which I would like to call your attention to; it is the fact that fogs are not generally very high above the water; that a vessel's masts sometimes project into a clear atmosphere above—that if a man is sent aloft, where, by the bye, one ought always to be, at least during the daytime, to look out for wrecks and rafts, or boats, he can often see the masts of approaching vessels, land, and other high objects. This is not generally thought of, even by seagoing people. A story is told of a captain, who was cruising off Wilmington, in the South, a few years ago, for the benefit of his health. At night, the vessels all hugged in close to the bar, to pick up excursion parties, who might be carrying out too much cotton. One morning (it was foggy) this officer decided, as he was very close in, to wait later than usual. Suddenly he heard the pleasant whistle of a shell, right between his masts; followed by another, with a slight improvement of aim. He politely requested one of his men to go aloft, and see what was the matter. This individual suddenly emerged into the clear sunlight, and took an instantaneous view of the Mound Battery, which was also enjoying a beautiful morning. It is needless to say that the vessel changed her range, and that the captain had learned a lesson.

The next subject is the consideration of what is being done on shore for the safety of the traveler.

The Light-house Service affords great protection. This service, although under the Treasury Department, is actually administered by the officers of the Navy and Army Engineer Corps. Admiral John Rodgers is at present the chairman of the board, which is made up of: three naval officers, two army officers, one ex-naval officer, and one scientist. The coast, rivers and lakes are divided into fifteen districts, each of which has a naval officer for its inspector, and an army engineer for its constructor. Other officers are detailed as assistants in the large districts. There are on the Atlantic coast 451 lights, 43 hot-air or steam fog-signals, 422 day beacons, and 2,610 buoys. On the Pacific coast there are, in all, 211 aids to navigation. We omit those on the rivers and lakes. There are 33 light-ships on outlying shoals and dangers.

If all these lights were of good quality, our coast would be fairly well lighted. There is one improvement that should be made, and would be, probably, if the funds were appropriated. Every light-house, and especially outlying light-ships, should be signal and telegraph stations. They would then be able to give warning of bad weather, and if a wreck occurred near them, or was likely to occur, they could signal for aid to the nearest port or life-saving station. Many valuable lives and cargoes are lost, when the timely arrival of a tug or ground tackle would have saved all.

The navy, with a large corps of officers and ships in every port of the globe, is continually collecting information which renders navigation more safe, and therefore preserves life. There are some ships on special duty surveying the coasts of countries which are either uninhabited, or too poor to do the work themselves.

The army, with its signal service and "Old Probabilities," warns the mariner of approaching bad weather, and allows him time to prepare for the fight.

The private enterprise of one of our journals has done much to save life in giving notice of the approaches of distant storms, and advocating the adoption of greater precautions in the building of ships.

The Coast Survey, with its efficient head, an ex-naval officer, and a large number of assistants, most of whom are naval officers, is constantly watching our coast, giving notice of shifting channels, and newly-discovered dangers, locating old ones which have been reported, and furnishing charts, which are guides to all the world approaching our shores.

In England, much is done to save life. Two great benevolent societies are at the head of the movement: the Royal Humane Society, instituted in 1774, to collect and circulate the most approved and effectual methods for recovering persons apparently drowned or dead; to suggest and provide suitable apparatus for, and bestow rewards on, those who assist in the preservation and restoration of life. The Queen is its patron; the Duke of Argyle its president. Connected with this society are many local ones or branches.

The Royal National Life-Boat Institution, incorporated in 1824, under the name of the "Royal National Institution for the Preservation of Life from Shipwreck," and changed to its present title by a new charter in 1854. The Duke of Northumberland is the president. This society, aided by sub-societies and donations, provides the life-boats and apparatus for the whole English coast. The boats are generally very large ones, some of them being propelled by steam. The English coast is, at most points, very high. It is indented with many small harbors. The boats are kept in these harbors. The population of the coast is much more numerous than ours especially the maritime portion of it. The crews—they have very large ones—are all made up of volunteers, who are paid while in service. If successful in saving life, they receive special pecuniary rewards. The boats and crews are managed by what are called "local committees," the coast-guard naval officer being by the constitution a member. Where the distance to be traveled is great, steam and sail are used. For line-throwing, the Boxer rocket is used. This is a large rocket, very similar to that used for war purposes; it is fired from a wooden trough, which gives its direction and the proper elevation; the line is attached to the rocket. The method of using the line, being identical with ours, will be explained in connection with our own service. In 1874, there were 240 boats belonging to this society. The donations to the society in 1873 amounted to £31,740. In that year it saved 668 lives, and alto-

Fig. 1.

Fig. 2.

Fig. 3.

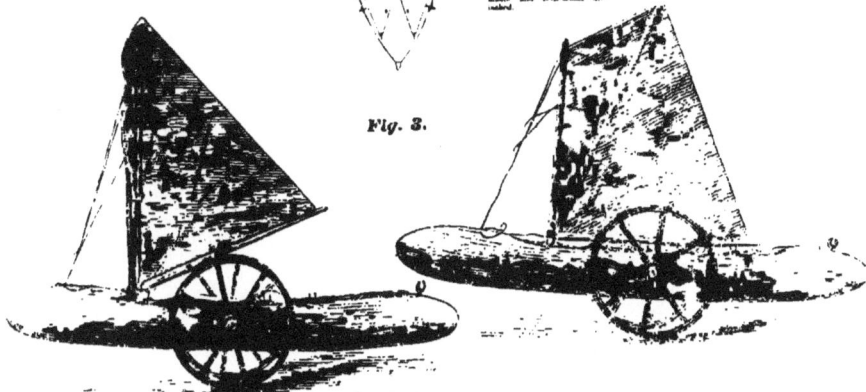

Fig. 1. LIFE BOAT ON CARRIAGE.
Fig. 2. PLAN OF LIFE BOAT.
Fig. 3. FORBES' LIFE BOAT ON WHEELS.

gether, up to that year, 22,153. It had granted 940 gold medals. These figures are for 1873–74, five years ago, and of course have increased very materially. The English claim that Lieutenant Bell, of the Royal Artillery, was the first to invent a means of conveying a line to a vessel, in 1791. Capt. Manby, R. N., was, however, the most successful of the early workers. His shot was used as late as 1862.

The British Society for the Encouragement of Arts, Manufactures and Commerce offered, in April, 1878, their gold medal to the person submitting the best means of saving life at sea when a vessel has to be abandoned suddenly, say with only five minutes' warning, the shore or other vessels being in sight. The decision has just been rendered in favor of cork mattresses faced with hair. I think that our cotton or deer hair mattresses are still more effective. It would be interesting to have this fact tested by a competitive trial, under the auspices of this society, or of the Life-Saving Benevolent one.

In France, the organization is somewhat similar to that of England, " The Société Centrale de Sauvetage des Naufragés" controlling the local boards. The French use the gun in preference to the rocket. They claim for M. Ducarne de Blangy the credit for having first invented a means of conveying a line by means of a projectile in 1790, and to a naval paymaster, named Broquet, the credit of having used a life kite successfully at Boulogne, in 1851.

In Russia, the service is managed by the Society for Assistance at Shipwrecks, under the patronage of the Grand Duchess Cæsarevna.

In Germany, Austria, Italy and Turkey, it is in the hands of similar societies.

In our own country, the first regularly organized society which undertook the duty of preserving and restoring life was the Massachusetts Humane Society; formed in 1786, and incorporated in 1791. It began the erection of huts, for the shelter and comfort of persons escaped from wrecked vessels upon exposed and desolate portions of the coast of Massachusetts, in 1789; the first one being erected on Lovell's Island, near Boston. It maintains at the present day eight such huts. Its first life-boat station was erected at Cohasset, 1807. Up to 1870, the Government appropriated in all

$35,000 to assist it. It had in 1876, with the assistance of the Government, 76 stations in hand.

The second society was, The Life-Saving Benevolent Society of New York, incorporated in 1849. Since that time it has rendered the greatest assistance in organizing the life-saving stations on the coasts of New York and New Jersey. It has awarded a large number of medals, and has encouraged the saving of life by volunteers. Its first president was Walter R. Jones, Esq.; its present one is Mr. John D. Jones. Its Vice-President, Mr. Royal Phelps. Mr. W. H. H. Moore, a member of our council, is one of its most zealous workers.

The Hon. William A. Newell, of New Jersey, a member of Congress in 1848, by a very strong speech, succeeded in getting an appropriation of $10,000 for surf boats and other appliances, to be used on the Jersey coast—from Sandy Hook to Little Egg Harbor. This amount was expended under the direction of officers detailed from the Revenue Marine Service and the New York Life Saving Benevolent Society.

Captain Ottinger, the inventor of the life-car, is represented in an old plate as experimenting with his life-saving gun and life-car, before a committee of the society—Messrs. Walter R. Jones and Lambert Suydam.

Eight stations were the result of this appropriation. Captains McGowan and Faunce also began their long and honorable connection with the service at this time.

March 3d, 1849, the Government made further appropriations for the erection of stations on the Long Island and Jersey coasts, so that at the end of the year about twenty-two stations were in operation. These stations were all manned by volunteer crews, and did excellent service.

Small appropriations were continued, and some few additional stations built; but the service did not really take any definite shape until the winter of 1870–71, when Congress made an appropriation of $200,000, and the present life-saving service was organized in 1872, under the Treasury Department. The work done by it seems almost incomprehensible, in view of the smallness of the appropriations. Even these appropriations are due to the untiring personal efforts of the Hon. Charles B. Roberts, of Maryland, and our townsman the Hon. S. S. Cox. To Hon. Sumner J. Kimball, a New Yorker, its Superintendent; Captains McGowan and Merriman, and Lieutenant Walker of the Revenue Marine, his senior assistants, the greatest credit is due. We know little of the difficulties which they have had to surmount. Results are the best means of measuring the value of an institution. Wherever the proper development has been afforded by legislative action, the success has been wonderful. The coast of North Carolina is the weakest point now, and Mr. Kimball is using every endeavor to get money to render it as humanly secure as the rest of the coast. Those who have the work in hand are fully competent to make the needed improvements, if only they have the means given them. They want assistance, and it would seem particularly appropriate that we, a society devoted to travel, should do what we can for them by word or deed.

The coast from Maine to Florida is divided into seven districts. Each district is in charge of a superintendent, and the large ones have, besides, an assistant. It is the duty of the superintendent to be always on the go, inspecting his crews and stations, and drilling his men.

The districts are as follows:

No. 1. Maine and New Hampshire, 6 Life-saving Stations, 1 building.

No. 2. Massachusetts, 14 Life-saving Stations, 1 building.

No. 3. Rhode Island and Long Island, 36 Life-saving Stations, 1 building.

No. 4. New Jersey, 40 Life-saving Stations.

No. 5. Delaware, Maryland, and Virginia to Cape Charles, 11 Life-saving Stations.

No. 6. Virginia from Cape Henry, and North Carolina, 10 Life-saving Stations, 13 building.

No. 7. Florida, 8 Houses of Refuge.

The Eighth, Ninth and Tenth Districts are on the lakes, and the Eleventh is the coast of California and Oregon, furnished with 11 life-boat stations.

There are three classes of stations:

First, Life-saving Stations—Situated in localities remote from settlements, furnished with every possible appliance for rescuing the ship-wrecked, and ministering to the immediate necessities and comforts of those saved. They also furnish quarters for the keepers and crews. On account of the limited means at the disposal of the management, the stations are manned only during the winter months. That this is unwise, although necessary, the Huron disaster showed. The crews now consist of six surf men besides the keeper.

Second, Life-boat Stations—Located near settlements where volunteer crews can easily be summoned. These are furnished with boats and such other appliances as the nature of their situation calls for. The stations of the Eleventh District are of this nature.

Third, Houses of Refuge—Situated in desolate localities, where the general state of the coast does not call for the use of the appliances furnished to the other class of stations. These are intended to afford shelter to those who may come ashore. They are provisioned and supplied with medicines, blankets, beds, &c. Small boats are placed in them, with which to reach points of safety or passing vessels. A keeper, with his family, resides in them.

Some of the stations are connected with the Weather Signal Service, by telegraph, some are being furnished with telephones, and are used as warning posts for passing vessels; this feature should be extended to all of them, and if the international code flags were added to the outfits, vessels could communicate with any part of the world from many points on the coast. A shore line of telegraph should connect the stations with each other, this line being besides fitted with alarm boxes on the poles, similar to those used by our fire department, would serve for the patrols to send in signals of distress from wherever they might be.

The small surf-boat is used at almost all the stations. Our coast is so sandy and rugged that it is impossible to transport life-boats weighing generally four or five thousand pounds. The surf men are also familiar with this style of boat, and seem to place more reliance in it than in any other. The smallness of the crews renders even this very difficult of transportation to any distance. Where they can be hired, horses are used, but where they are most wanted they cannot be obtained. It is recommended that four horses be kept at the stations on the most exposed and desolate parts of the coast. The patrols could ride two of these horses, the other two being always in reserve to bring out the apparatus.

Fig. 1.

Fig. 2.

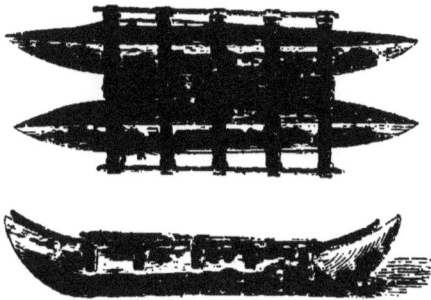

Fig. 1. EXTERIOR VIEW OF LIFE SAVING STATION.
Fig. 2. RIDER LIFE RAFT.

The men, as we have before stated, are employed for only a part of the year. This necessitates the breaking in of new crews every season. The pay is small and the work most arduous, which prevents men from reshipping. It is now proposed to regularly enlist the men, employing them in the off months in drilling, making a coast road, building stations, repairing apparatus, putting up telegraphs, and patrolling the coast, in case of a possible accident, or to prevent smuggling. The crew, as it now stands, is too small. Two men are always on patrol; in case of an alarm, one or both of these will be absent. The beats at present, in some localities, are longer than can possibly be watched by one man, often reaching a length of eight miles. Then, again, no lee-way is left for the sick list, or unavoidable absence. By a regular system of enlistment good crews could be obtained from districts where plenty of men are to be found, and transferred to those where the material is poor.

The appliances furnished at a complete station are:

A surf-boat fully equipped, boat carriage, mortar and appliances, pin board with line, sand tarpaulin and pegs, whip and hawser. Sand anchor, tackle and crutch.

Signal flags, lanterns and coston lights.

Beach light.

Life car, life raft and breeches buoy, medicines, tools, provisions, blankets and beds, also

A hand cart, in which those of the above-named articles, except the boat, that are required at the scene of action, are conveyed.

The boat is used when advisable; chief reliance, however, is placed in the line.

The method of proceeding is as follows: three hundred fathoms of line are coiled on a pin board, the different layers running clear of each other, and paying off the pins. This board is covered by a box, when wanted for use. The box is turned over, the pin-board being carefully withdrawn, guided by the false bottom. This leaves the line faked in the box. This box is placed to windward of the mortar, and the end of the line is attached, either by means of a spiral spring, or directly, to the projectile. The latter method has proved the most certain; care is taken to wet the end of the line to prevent its burning. The projectile is elongated in shape, the line coming to the outer end, which protrudes from the muzzle. On starting, the projectile first turns over, so as to bring the line to the rear. The mortar is trained so as to point between the masts of the vessel. Should the first shot miss, the line is run in and coiled on the tarpaulin, which is pinned down to the ground with tent pegs.

The line, having reached the vessel, is hauled upon by those on board, the whip block having been attached to the shore end. Attached to the block, is a board or bottle with directions in English, French and German for making it fast. The block is made fast as high above the deck as possible, by means of its tail. The next operation is the hauling out of the hawser; done by those on shore, who have first taken the precaution to join the two ends of the whip. The hawser is made fast to the mast above the tail block. As soon as "all fast" is signalled from the vessel, the shore end is hauled hand taut. The sand anchor, two pieces of heavy plank crossed and fitted with an eye-bolt at the intersection, is planted in a trench. The crutch is then set up; the hawser being taken over its crotch. The tackle is clapped on to the hawser, and hooked to the sand anchor. If the vessel is rolling, it is necessary to tend the tackle, if not, it is set taut and belayed. The life-car, which is like a small life-boat with a cover, is then suspended to the hawser, hauled out to the wreck by means of the whip, the bight of which is made fast to a traveler; when loaded, it is hauled ashore again by the other part of the whip.

The car is necessary when there are landsmen, women, children or invalids to be conveyed ; for seamen the breeches buoy is used. This is a large cork life preserver with a pair of canvas breeches attached, the man sitting in it. This buoy may be used on the whip alone if necessary.

The rescued persons once ashore are taken to the station and cared for.

The records of the service show this year that within the limits of the operations of the service 171 disasters to vessels. On board these vessels were 1,557 persons. The estimated value of the vessels is $1,879,063 and that of their cargoes $745,672, making the total value of the property involved $2,624,735. The number of lives saved was 1,331 and the number lost 226. Of the latter number 183 perished in the disaster to the United States steamer *Huron* and the

Fig. 1.

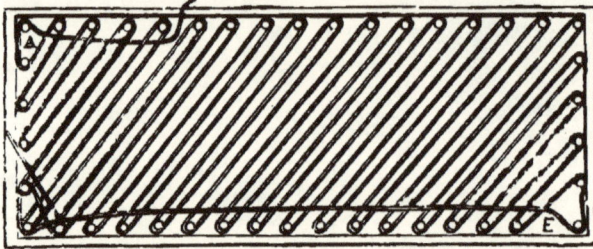

Fig. 2.

Fig. 3.

Fig. 4.

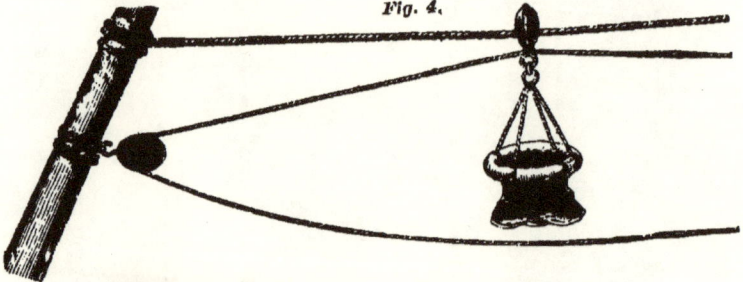

Fig. 5.

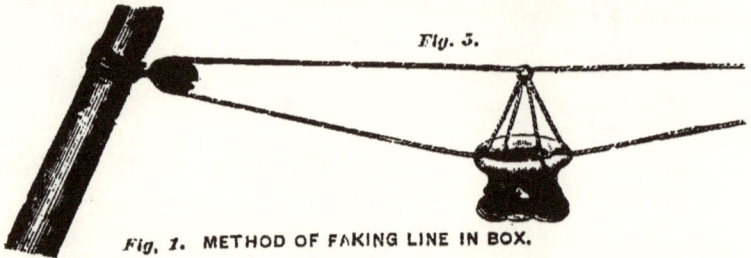

Fig. 1. METHOD OF FAKING LINE IN BOX.

Fig. 2. METALLIC LIFE CAR.

Fig. 3. SECTION THROUGH METALLIC LIFE CAR.

Fig. 4. BREECHES BUOY USED WITH HAWSER.

Fig. 5. BREECHES BUOY USED ON SHIP.

steamship *Metropolis*—98 in the former and 85 in the latter. The number of shipwrecked persons sheltered and succored at the stations during the year was 425, the total number of days' relief afforded them being 832. The total value of property saved is estimated at $1,097,375, and the amount lost at $1,527,360. The number of disasters involving the total loss of vessels and cargoes was 595. These statistics show that the disasters of the present year were greater in number and severer in character than the service has ever before encountered, a fact established by the record of 171 disasters within life-saving limits against 134, the highest number of any former year, and of 59 vessels and cargoes totally lost, in contrast with the highest antecedent record of 34. A large proportion of the loss of life is made up, as before stated, of the 183 persons who perished at the wrecks of the *Huron* and *Metropolis*, the first wreck occurring before the opening of the stations under the provisions of law, and the latter between two stations at such a distance from either as to greatly hinder successful operations, conditions which had long been indicated by the officers in charge of the service as pregnant with fatality. There were four other wrecks, involving the loss of ten lives, which occurred when the stations were closed, and one other disaster, involving the loss of four lives, happened at a distance which made prompt assistance impossible. The General Superintendent shows that the number of lives lost fairly and legitimately within the scope of the effective operations of the service was but twenty-nine, and further shows that this loss of life was unpreventable by human efforts. The particulars of each case are given in detail.

Thus far the lines have been sent from the shore to the vessel, and Lieutenant D. A. Lyle, of the Army Ordnance Corps, who has been for some time experimenting for the service, has succeeded in producing a bronze, muzzle-loading, smooth-bore gun, of which he recommends three calibres 2 in., 2.5 in., 3 in., to be used according to the ranges required in the different parts of our coast. This gun with its carriage and shot weighs a little over 200 lbs, and has reached a maximum range of 695 yards, far more than any other has ever succeeded in doing. The shots weigh 13, 19 and 23 lbs. respectively. The line used is waterproof braided linen thread, very carefully selected, made by the Silver Lake Company. One of the great advantages of this gun and projectile is that it does not allow the line to sag to leeward as much as its predecessors, and therefore gives greater accuracy. Rifled guns cannot be used with lines, as the rifled motion would twist them and cause them to foul. Mr. Edmund S. Hunt, of Weymouth, Massachusetts, has invented an apparatus for throwing lines, which, under certain circumstances, principally on account of its portability and compactness, might be of great service. It consists of two hollow metallic cylinders, closed at one end. In each of these is coiled away part of the line to be thrown. One of these cylinders, containing enough line to reach the object, is loaded into a very light gun, also of his invention; the other is held in the hand of the operator. When the gun is fired, the cylinder leaves it and turns over, paying out the line as it goes. If there should not be enough line in it to reach the object, the line in the second cylinder acts as a reserve. The theory is very good, and if the gun had been as good the system would probably have been adopted. You have all seen a hose-cart at fires. When the hose is first attached to the hydrant, or engine, and the reel dragged away, paying out the hose as it goes, it is an easy operation; but if the hose-cart is taken to the scene of the fire several blocks away, and then the hose unreeled by hand, and the end dragged to the hydrant, the operation is much more difficult. This is the principle of Hunt's shot, and that of all instruments of a similar nature where the line is payed out from the movable body, and not dragged by it.

In all the life-saving services to which we have referred, the lines have been sent from the shore to the ship; it is conceded by all that this is not the proper way. The line should come from the ship; but, until we can force shipowners and governments to provide their vessels with some means of sending lines, and even having them to send, we must continue this method.

When a ship goes ashore the wind is generally blowing hard on shore, and the sea setting in the same direction; it is true that there is generally more or less of a current running parallel with the beach; therefore, from the ship we have two elements acting in our favor. From the shore we have this against us. From the shore we have only a small target, the ship, to fire at. If she comes in and strands bows on, it is smaller, even, than when she presents her

Fig. 3,

Fig. 4,

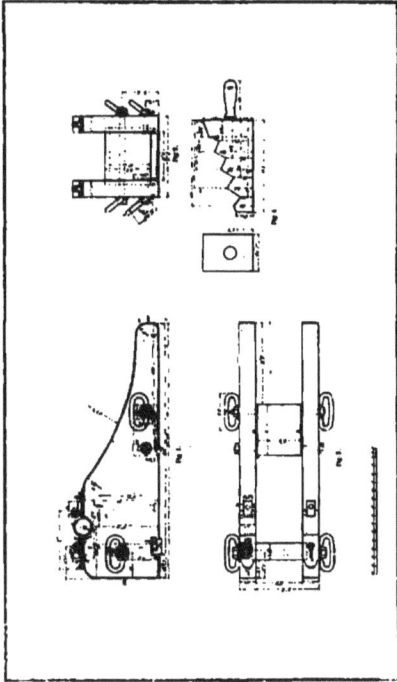

Fig. 4. FAKING BOX.

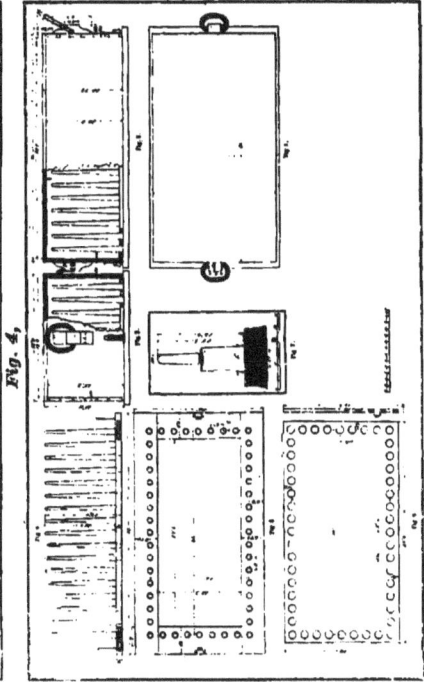

Fig. 3. CARRIAGE.

Fig. 1.

Fig. 2,

Fig. 2. PROJECTILE.

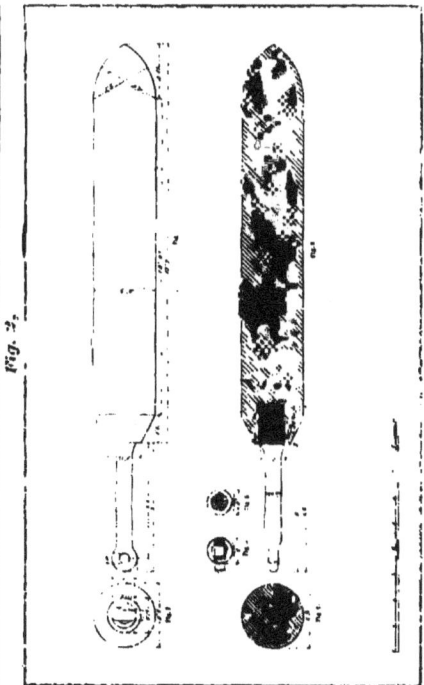

Fig. 1. LYLE GUN.

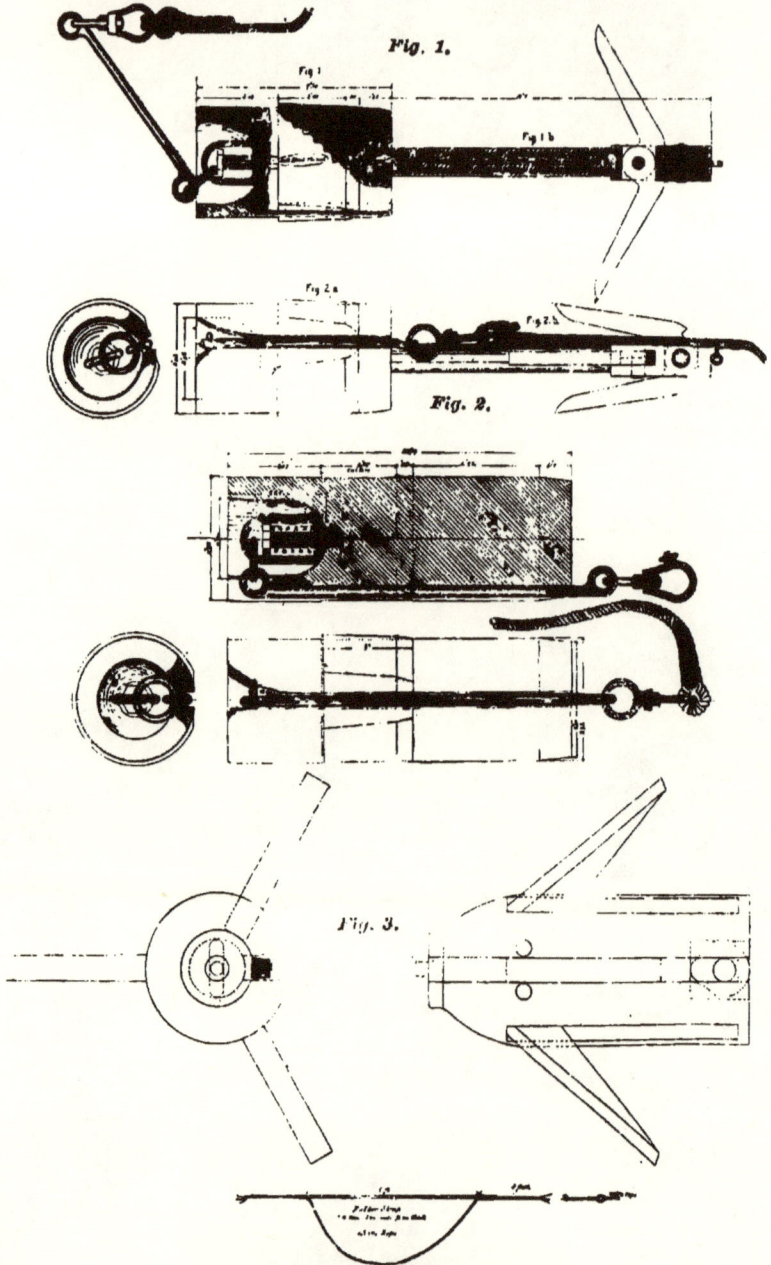

Fig. 1. FOLGER'S GRAPNELL SHOT.
Fig. 2. FOLGER'S LIFE SAVING SHOT.
Fig. 3. CHANDLER'S ANCHOR SHOT.

broadside to us. Sending a line to a ship's bows is a very difficult operation, under the most favorable circumstances, especially so in winter, when the bows are generally covered with an armor of ice. On a dark stormy night, or in the fog, the ship may not be visible at all. From the ship we have the whole continent as a target.

An apparatus on the ship would be at hand, and could be started immediately; on the shore it may have to be brought miles, under the greatest difficulties, consuming sometimes hours of precious time. Furthermore, on some coasts there are no life-saving appliances to be brought, and the ship would always have hers with her.

The following are some of the methods that might be used from the ship:

A life-saving gun, similar to those used on shore, which would also answer as a signal gun for a merchant vessel.

A man-of-war could use her own guns if proper shot were provided. Capt. Ralph Chandler, U. S. N., has been experimenting lately, and has obtained excellent results with our guns, using a shot which is fitted with arms forming the flukes of an anchor; these fasten themselves in the ground or rocks where they land, so that the line may be hauled upon without the aid of persons on shore. This would be a great advantage on uninhabited coasts.

Lieut.-Comd'r. W. M. Folger has also been experimenting in the same line, and has obtained excellent results.

If a shot is not provided, a length of chain can be wound up into a ball of the proper size, and thus secured the line is made fast to the end of the chain. An empty shell with the line toggled in the fuse-hole might serve.

The objections to using a gun would be that when there was much motion on, or the seas washing over the vessel, or the vessel on her beam-ends, it might not be possible to get it in the proper position for firing. About eighty per cent. of vessels that go broadside on, heel to seaward.

Rockets might be used with good effects. With as weak a rocket as our common signal one, I sent a line four hundred feet last year. A small line fastened to the ramrod of a musket might be used for short distances. Captain Nares, of the English Navy, known to you probably in connection with the voyage of the *Challenger* and the last Arctic expedition, proposes a large kite, made of canvas and spars and fitted with two lines, so that it can be guided up or down. To this I have added an anchor-tail. Such a kite would also be of use in communicating between vessels at sea where it was dangerous to lower a boat. A line fastened to a box or barrel might drift ashore.

An expert swimmer in a life-preserver, or on a mattress or bolsa might reach the shore in safety with the end of the line, if better means were not at hand.

Capt. James E. Jouett and Lieut.-Comd'r W. B. Hoff, of the Navy, have invented an apparatus which will probably be adopted in the service. It consists of a float carrying a reel, on which can be wound 6,000 feet of line. At the forward end is a large rectangular shield. This shield is so placed that, no matter how the float turns, one corner will always be up to act as a sail and one down to act as an anchor. The weight of the apparatus is about 200 pounds. It is intended to be carried one on each side of the vessel, hung over the side at sea, the end of the line being made fast on board. No matter how the vessel grounds, one at least will be in position for use. It is let go by a detaching apparatus and starts for the shore paying out the line, which, being heavier than water, sinks and lies along the bottom; this prevents drifting. As the line pays out from the float there is no retardation. The sail-point is acted on by the wind, which would force the whole machine across any moderate coast-current. When it gets into shallow water the lower point keeps it from being carried back with the undertow; each succeeding wave carrying it higher on the beach, where it is picked up by those on shore. If the coast is uninhabited it acts in the same manner as the anchor-shot already referred to. A ring-buoy is to be attached to this float, so that it can be used at sea to succor a person overboard.

Another float is that of Dr. Newell, of Asbury Park, New Jersey. This is a cone, which floats on its side, point foremost. Near the rear end is a concave diaphragm, in the centre of which is secured a bar which passes to the rear through a cross-support and projects some distance beyond, having an eye in its end; to this eye is attached the end of the line. The buoy is put overboard, and the wind

Fig. 1.

Fig. 2.

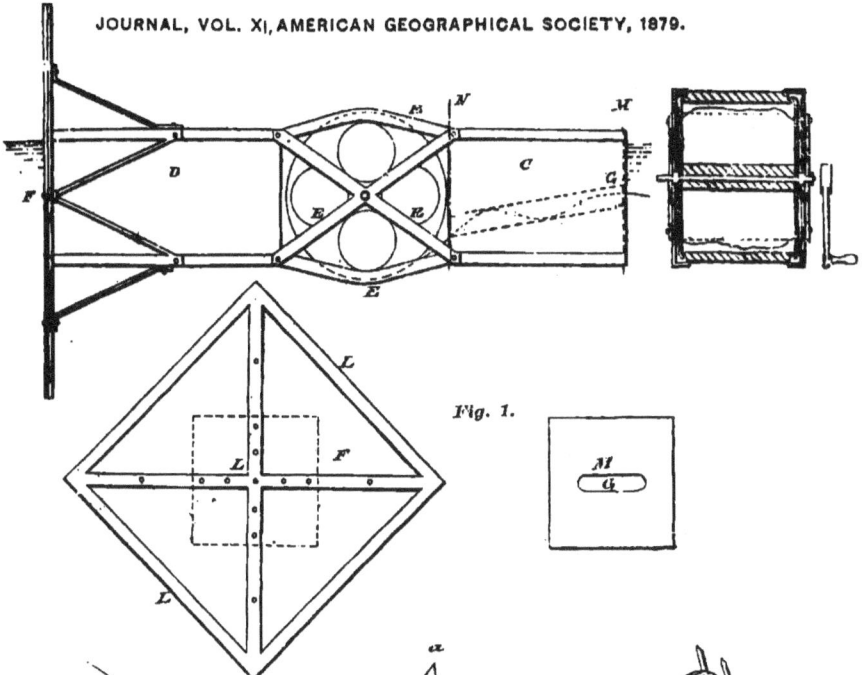

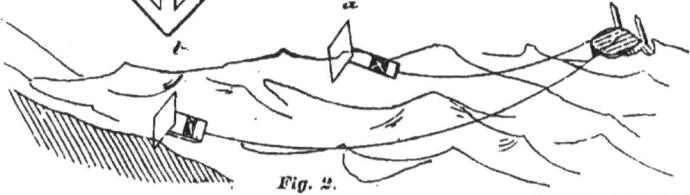

Fig. 1. JOUETT—HOFF APPARATUS.
Fig. 2. LIFE SAVING BY MEANS OF ROCKET AND BREECHES BUOY.

and sea acting on its rear end it is driven towards the shore. When its reaches the coast-current it is steered across by hauling on or slacking the line from on board. This causes the current to act against one or the other interior faces of the cone and makes it act like the swing-bridges still to be seen on some of our Western rivers. The line once ashore, there is a good chance of saving all hands. Of course it would be better if the ship carried and sent ashore the whip and hawser. A life-car or buoy could easily be contrived from the means at hand.

And now, gentlemen and ladies, as I know you would like to have a look at the practical working of our system, let me invite you to put on your warmest clothing, your waterproofs and your thick boots, and come with me this evening to the lonely coast of North Carolina, not quite so lonely as it was on the night the *Huron* was lost. The patrol man of the nearest station, which is eight miles off, is now there. But see, he is looking seaward. He thought just now that he saw the gleam of a light. He was right. Almost blinded by the salt spray from the sea mixed with sand from the beach, he is able to make out a vessel's lights, and to add to his certainty, there goes her gun. She is heading right in for the breakers and will ground in a few seconds. The patrol burns his Coston light to show them that they are seen. More he cannot do until he summons assistance. He starts for the station, and after weary hours of toiling, which can only be appreciated by those who have tried such a journey on our coast in a winter's storm, he reaches his destination. The alarm is given, and in a few minutes the crew start with their apparatus. Six men, all told, one being far away to the westward on patrol, and cannot be recalled, and one of this small number is already exhausted by his previous endeavors, dragging a hand-cart weighing, with its load, over 1,700 lbs., almost 280 lbs. per man, 180 being the utmost allowed, on level roads, as the traction of one man, with the wheels, whose tires are five inches broad, sinking several inches into the sand. After tugging through sand, and floundering in mud, sometimes entirely halted by the storm, at all times straining every muscle, they reach the scene of disaster. There they find that hours before the vessel has gone to pieces, and all that they can do is to save a few corpses from the surf. Could human beings have done more with the means at hand ? And when we know that these men get for such work a sum of $1.33 a day for five months in the year, can we say that they have not fully earned it ? Yet with all this, to morrow the opinion will go forth, from the pens of a hundred well-clothed and comfortably-lodged gentlemen, that the U. S. Life-saving Service is a fraud, the organization is bad, the officers are inefficient, the crews are poor, and the patrolmen negligent in the performance of their duties. Now, should these same gentlemen devote their energies to assisting the Service, instead of belittling it, in the popular opinion, how much could be gained. The lesson would be taken to heart; public sentiment would come to the aid of the organization; appropriations would be increased, and everything done to make such another accident impossible. . With such aid to carry out the plans already matured, we should have another story. The patrolman, two, or at most three miles from his station, would have dismounted from his horse; going to the nearest telegraph pole, he would have sent in the alarm; burnt his light; and watched for the line to come ashore; he would then have attached the line to his horse, and with his aid have hauled in the whip. In the meantime, the crew, with the apparatus drawn by two good horses, would have arrived by an excellent coast road made by the men in summer. The hawser would then be sent out, or one might be hauled ashore from the ship if it could be gotten at on board. The car then attached and hauled out, the horses being used to assist, it would then come ashore; and when opened who knows but what young Solon, son of Congressman Solon, and Mr. Hardcash, the great banker and beloved friend of Senator Demosthenes, might not be found comfortably ensconced therein ? What a comforting thing it would be to Messrs. Demosthenes and Solon to think that they had both voted for the increased appropriation, and a bill for the further perfecting of the United States Life-saving Service. Who knows but we ourselves, or our friends, may some day need the life-car ?

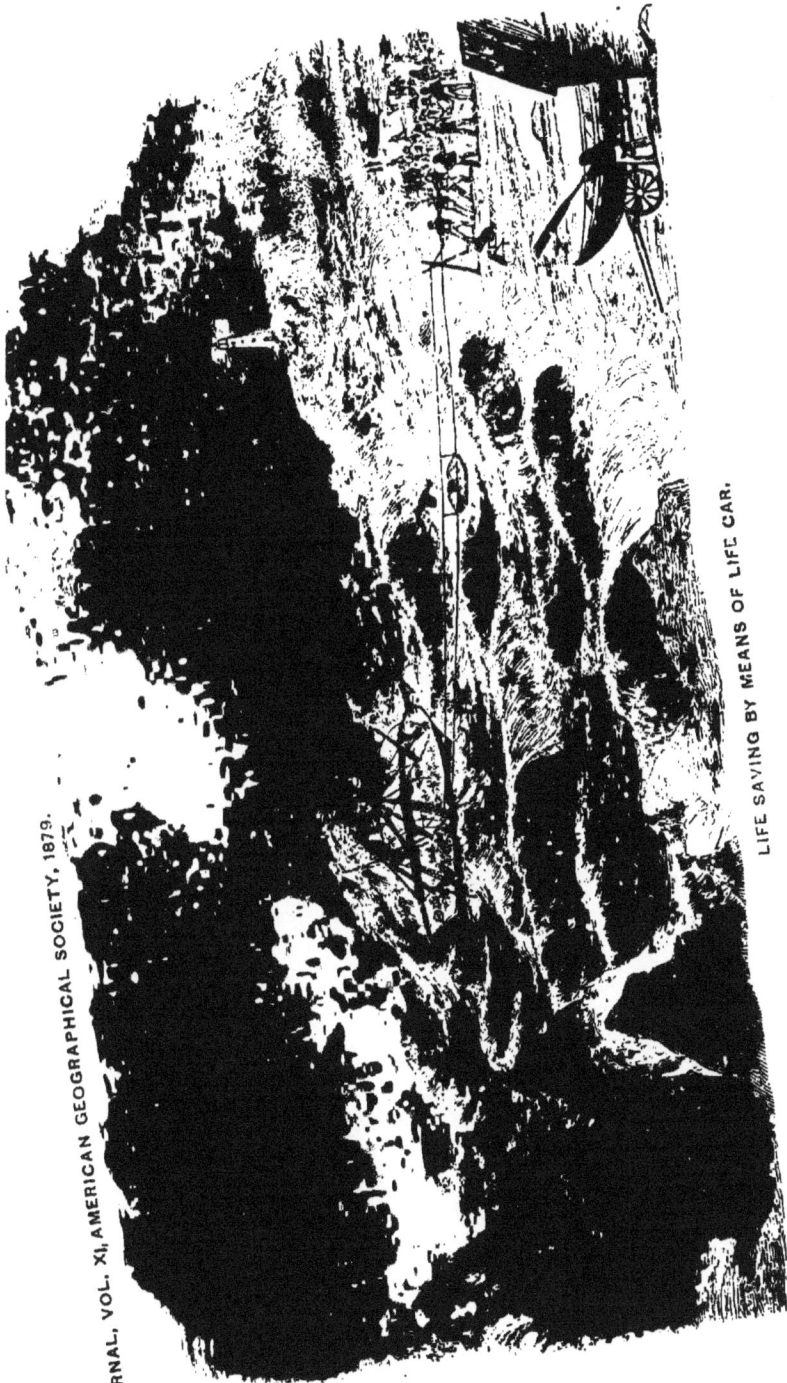

LIFE SAVING BY MEANS OF LIFE CAR.

www.ingramcontent.com/pod-product-compliance
Lightning Source LLC
Chambersburg PA
CBHW022153090426
42742CB00010B/1494